The light sees the light in you, keep shining!

Ana Castillo Jiménez

Metamorphosis

Unveiling My Inner Light

Ana Castillo Jiménez

Metamorphosis

Unveiling My Inner Light

Metamorphosis: Unveiling My Inner Light

Copyright © 2023 Ana Castillo Jimenez

All rights reserved.

No part of this book may be reproduced, stored in a retrieval system, or transmitted in any form or by any means, electronic, mechanical, photocopying, recording, or otherwise, without express written permission from the publisher.

ISBN-13: 979-8-9888048-1-9

Cover design by: Ana Castillo Jimenez

Within each of us, there is a tale untold,
A personal metamorphosis waiting to unfold.

Our lives are ongoing anthologies,
And we each get to write our own stories.

This book is dedicated to those trapped in their shells,
May it remind you of the beauty that within you dwells.

Contents

Prologue	1
Part I: The Egg	**3**
Mental Shell	5
Protective Illusions	7
Shedding the Critic	9
Mirrors of Self-Reflection	11
Maturing Mindfulness	13
Intention's Guiding Light	15
Majestic Consciousness	17
Embryonic Diapause	19
Hatching	21
Part II: The Larva	**23**
Learning to Crawl	25
Calm Amidst the Storm	27
Caterpillar's Call	29
Larval Harmony	31
Gentle Warrior	33
Molting	35
Restoring Energy	37
Bonds of Belonging	39
Pre-Pupation	41

Part III: The Pupa — 43

Awakening Chrysalis — 45

Whispers of Transformation — 47

Ethereal Beginnings — 49

Gratitude's Radiance — 51

Pupal Love — 53

Transcending Perspective — 55

Wing Development — 57

Authentic Coloring — 59

Eclosion — 61

Part IV: The Adult — 63

Through the Cocoon's Veil — 65

Celestial Wings — 67

Colors in Flight — 69

Rise of the Monarch — 71

Unveiling Splendor — 73

Eternal Beauty — 75

Flying Toward Destiny — 77

Graceful Evolution — 79

Unfolding the Mystery — 81

Epilogue — 83

Acknowledgments — 85

Prologue

I am like an egg, fragile and small,
With endless potential, awaiting my call.

I have been trapped within this egg's shell,
My thoughts and emotions have created a cell.

Held tight within anxiety's embrace,
I live with my shadows, lost in space.

I have been sitting in the darkness, lonely and confined,
Desperate for a way out, with no light in my mind.

But within this fragile chamber, whispers echo clear,
Of memories, thoughts, and moments that I hold dear.

I know there is more to life than this cold darkness,
If only I could find a way out of my personal madness.

I'm tired of going through life this way,
I'm tired of waiting to be happy someday.

If I want to get better, I must let the healing begin,
By letting go of the past and releasing the pain within.

For in the depths of my soul lies a desire to be,
To enjoy every moment as I live wild and free.

The answers lie within a sacred domain,
Where authenticity begins to reign.

Through trials and tests, I'll come to know,
The answers I seek that will help me grow.

The pain I feel tells me it's time to change,
It's time to step into a life that may feel strange.

Metamorphosis

I know within me lies the power to thrive,
As I spread my wings and truly come alive.

In the captivating dance of nature's art,
A metaphor unfolds, reflecting my heart.

A caterpillar's transformation, profound and true,
Mirroring the journey that awaits me and you.

Contained in a tiny egg, potential lies in wait,
Dreaming of wings destined by fate.

Within each of us, brilliance yearns to be,
It is the untapped light, the essence of being free.

Embarking on a personal exploration, I shall go,
Through the stages of metamorphosis, finding my glow.

The egg, the larva, the pupa, and the butterfly,
Will each guide me through this metaphoric sky.

I want to take back control over my life,
By learning how to deal with suffering and strife.

Self-discovery and acceptance will pave the way,
As I uncover the beauty that within me lays.

I know there is a spark within me, a piece of the divine,
And it has been patiently waiting for its time to shine.

I have kept it locked alongside the secrets that I keep,
And it comes out to haunt me when I try to sleep.

It longs to be free, to let itself be shown,
Asking me to leave behind this cell that I've known.

I want to leave this egg so that I may evolve,
But first, there are a few things I must resolve.

PART I

The Egg

"We delight in the beauty of the butterfly, but rarely admit the changes it has gone through to achieve that beauty."

— Maya Angelou

"We are but small butterflies in the garden of life."

— Carston D. Roach

The Egg

Mental Shell

In the lobes of my mind, I reside,
Trapped by the walls I have built inside.

Beyond this shell constructed by fears,
There are dreams that have laid dormant for years.

In a labyrinth of thoughts, I dwell,
Imprisoned within my self-made cell.

Afraid to break free, afraid to dream,
Caught in the current of a silent stream.

I feel the need to make myself small,
So that those around me can feel tall.

For years, I've tried to fit in to please them all,
But in doing so, I've ignored my soul's call.

I no longer recognize the reflection I see,
A stranger stares back at me, longing to be free.

Insecurities cast shadows upon each hopeful day,
Fueled by concerns that tend to lead me astray.

Limiting beliefs have kept me in a bind,
They constrict my thoughts and leave me confined.

Self-imposed restraints tighten their embrace,
Holding me back from the boundless space.

I have been boxed in by societal norms,
And I now yearn to embody my proper form.

A prisoner of worries, judgments, and doubts,
My spirit is tired, and now seeks a way out.

Metamorphosis

Negative thoughts, like clouds they loom,
Casting darkness upon my once vibrant bloom.

The weight of opinions and rejection I bear,
Feeling hopeless, like there is no repair.

But within this eggshell, I must now concede,
The power to dream lies within my own seed.

For there is more to life, I clearly see,
Beyond the confines of my mind's decree.

A voice within me longs to spread its wings,
To explore this vast world and the joy it can bring.

I have the strength to leave my fears behind,
And to let my aspirations freely unwind.

I don't want to keep living this life I've known,
So, I'll reclaim my spirit and let my light be shown.

By leaving behind compulsive thinking,
I will be able to end my habitual worrying.

In the vast expanse of life's grand design,
I will break the shell and finally be fine.

No longer chained by others' opinions or views,
I can find liberation in being unapologetically true.

In daring to break free, I will find my true worth,
Unveiling the beauty that lies within my birth.

The light within keeps me orbiting with its gravity,
As it invites me on a voyage of self-discovery.

No more shrinking, no more hiding away,
It is time to find the courage to seize the day.

The Egg

Protective Illusions

Within the egg I've called home, illusions reside,
Self-imposed beliefs that have trapped me inside.

Whispers in the dark keep me up at night,
A web of lies that dampens my light.

Limiting and constricting, they mutter in my ear,
"I am not enough," a mantra I've come to fear.

I've yearned to be wanted, desired, and seen,
Thinking if I were different, I'd fit in the scene.

"If only I were better," my thoughts then say,
Leaving me to wonder if I will ever find my way.

Stronger, smarter, skinnier, prettier, or funnier,
These elusive qualities I believe would make me better.

But they are just illusions, merely smoke and mirrors,
False narratives that have held me captive for years.

In the pursuit of perfection, I've lost sight,
Of the beauty within, waiting to shine bright.

How can I expect others to cherish and want me,
If I don't grant myself the compassion I need to be free?

It is time to put an end to this cycle of despair,
To give myself love and care so that my heart may repair.

I can learn to honor and love who I am,
By rewriting the beliefs in my mental program.

I will shatter these illusions and break them apart,
So that I can love myself fully and ignite my own heart.

Metamorphosis

My fears and beliefs have kept me confined,
But I now realize they're all creations of my mind.

They are just thoughts; ideas that deceive,
No longer will I listen, for it is time to believe:

I am enough, worthy of love and delight,
And I don't need others to tell me what is "right."

It is time to move on, to seek something new,
To rewrite the script and let my spirit breakthrough.

I am more than the sum of my fears and doubts,
I am a warrior, ready to rise and shout.

The thoughts that once plagued me will lose their sway,
For they don't get to decide how I live each day.

Identifying limiting beliefs, I shed their weight,
As I step into a future where my dreams await.

It is time to move on with life, to look at what's ahead,
To believe in myself, regardless of what others have said.

With mindfulness as my guide, I'll witness each thought,
As I separate the truth from the illusions I've bought.

I will remove the ideas that no longer serve me,
I will replace them with self-love and allow myself to be.

By letting go of what does not agree,
I make room for what I wish to see.

I am ready to delve within and start anew,
Embracing the authenticity that shines through.

No longer defined by what others may see,
I am rewriting the script and setting myself free.

The Egg

Shedding the Critic

Beyond illusions, there is a voice in my mind,
An inner critic that is relentless and unkind.

It fuels depression and anxiety, draining my energy,
As it comes up with stories about how life "should be."

My thoughts spiral out of control and wildly roam,
My emotions scatter and leave me feeling alone.

I've sought solace in doctors and prescriptions,
But overlooked the power of my own convictions.

Through the dark, I can see with crystal-clear clarity,
That these thoughts and feelings do not define me.

No longer shall I count on external might,
To fix the turmoil, to make me feel all right.

Instead, I will inquire with gentle curiosity,
What my thoughts and feelings are trying to tell me.

In my mind, a friend is waiting to be found,
Whispering wisdom, hoping I will come around.

Into the depths of dark thoughts, I will delve,
To decipher the messages they long to tell.

Instead of fighting the current within,
I will let it carry me to where peace begins.

No longer will mental concepts keep me in a bind,
For I know I am more than the thoughts in my mind.

With self-compassion, I will heal and repair,
As I go through my journey with love and care.

Metamorphosis

I am ready to venture into the void inside of me,
Ready to face the suffering that drowns me like the sea.

I will turn my darkness into light,
So that I can rest in peace at night.

By nurturing my body, mind, and soul,
I will find the strength to reclaim control.

No longer at odds, no longer apart,
I will unite the fragments and mend my heart.

I can't keep ignoring the feelings that hurt,
For they contain a truth that's sweeter than dessert.

Slowly but surely, the tide will turn,
And to my true self, I will return.

The inner critic's voice will be blown by the breeze,
As it transforms into a friend who brings me ease.

Within the chaos, harmony will rise,
Revealing the beauty beneath my disguise.

I will honor my values and nurture my soul,
Until my mind and body both become whole.

In being honest with myself about how I feel,
I take the first step in learning how to heal.

I may not know why I feel what I do,
And not knowing is okay too.

I know these feelings won't last,
And soon, my sky won't be overcast.

I must learn to let my walls come down,
So that I may walk upon higher ground.

The Egg

Mirrors of Self-Reflection

After taming the inner critic, I embark on a quest,
Using meditative mindfulness to bring my soul rest.

In the depths of stillness, I find my retreat,
An inner island where the waters are sweet.

Delving inside is a coveted communion,
The mirrors in my soul display a reunion.

I feel both light and darkness within,
The boundary between them is paper thin.

Through the veil of thoughts, I venture to see,
The essence of my being, the authentic me.

I travel to the place where my true self resides,
A dreamer, a lover, and a fighter of tides.

In the sanctuary of silence, I shed the false self,
As I unravel the layers and find my inner wealth.

I see the strength that lies within my core,
Allowing me to crack the shell that held me before.

I have been afraid of the world, for it is unknown,
But now it calls out to me, promising I won't be alone.

It calls me forth to share my inner light,
To illuminate the darkness and soar in flight.

Instead of going where others might lead,
I will forge a new path at my own speed.

With a pen in hand, I pour out my soul,
Ink upon paper, thoughts begin to unroll.

Metamorphosis

Words flow freely, like a river's gentle stream,
Guiding me closer to my soul's sacred dream.

Upon tear-stained pages, my essence is bared,
A moment of reflection where I am truly aware.

Secrets spread upon sheets, an intimate conversation,
As I navigate the depths through my soul's exploration.

In the realm of journaling, I find my melody,
A tune that my mind, body, and spirit begin to study.

I continue my journey with pen and heart aligned,
One whispers to the other and the truth is defined.

Mirrors of self-reflection, portals to the soul,
Reveal the dreams that yearn to be whole.

For the answers reside within my own heart,
As it guides my steps toward a hopeful start.

In a world of constant change, it's hard to just be,
I am lucky the only thing I need to be is me.

In the stillness, my dreams become clear,
And I step into a world of things I hold dear.

I read each page carefully, every word a step to take,
As I learn more about myself, my spirit feels awake.

Through meditation and journaling, it is easier to see,
The essence of the person that I am meant to be.

By wearing my heart on my sleeve,
I know there is nothing I can't achieve.

With rhymes and metaphors, I navigate the way,
And I discover my light as I illuminate each day.

The Egg

Maturing Mindfulness

In seeing my true self, I find my grace,
And I accept each moment at my own pace.

Distractions dissolve as I turn my gaze,
To what is in front of me, in conscious ways.

I release tension with each beat of my heart,
Slowing my breathing as I prepare for a new start.

No longer lost in the chaos of my mind,
I cut through the noise and stillness I find.

In the rhythm of life's unfolding dance,
I turn to the present and give it a chance.

With focused intention, I take a vow,
To bring my attention to the here and now.

The present moment is all there is,
In accepting where I am, I find my bliss.

Instead of worrying about what likely won't occur,
I accept situations, the way they are and how they were.

Putting away screens that beg for attention,
I seek clarity through my own perception.

I breathe in the sun as it shines on my skin,
And breathe out the darkness I've been holding within.

With mindfulness as a partner, guiding my way,
In each moment, I choose to consciously stay.

I untangle the webs of past and future,
And ground myself firmly as a present explorer.

Metamorphosis

As I eat, I savor each bite that I take,
Thankful for the nourishment that others forsake.

With each step I take on this earthly ground,
I feel the universe, the energy that is all around.

When I speak, my words carry intention,
They flow with loving grace, my truest expression.

Aware of the impact my actions may impart,
I choose love and kindness right from the start.

For it's not about the path that I choose to pursue,
What matters is how I show up in all that I do.

Whether easy or tough, big or small,
I give life my all as I receive the call.

With mindful awareness, I honor each day,
And seize every moment that comes my way.

By loving the present moment, I find my anchor,
And I stop being concerned with the past and future.

Through mindfulness, I find the key,
To unlock the richness of truly being free.

With gratitude, I cherish this precious art,
A dance of consciousness, a work of the heart.

Stillness allows me to see beyond my personality,
It brings inner peace as I meet my true identity.

So, let the world around me spin and sway,
In the stillness within, I choose to stay.

With each breath I take, I am closer to grace,
As I awaken and find my sacred space.

The Egg

Intention's Guiding Light

Residing in inner stillness, I find my delight,
As my soul guides me forward with its radiant light.

A vision forms within and improves my clarity,
As I take the following steps on a path meant just for me.

With my heart as my compass, I set my course anew,
Knowing what I seek, fulfilment comes into view.

I set sail toward a life that is no longer blue,
And fight for the dreams that I wish to pursue.

I get to choose the emotions I allow in,
So, I will choose the ones that help me win.

I choose gratitude, and I choose love,
As I allow their light to fill me from above.

I choose to believe life is working out for me,
Regardless of what others may think or see.

I choose a life of abundance and inner peace,
And a sense of purpose that will never cease.

I envision a life where my light shines true,
A life where my confidence breaks through.

The shell that protected me will hold me no more,
It is time to break free so that my dreams may soar.

Each dream becomes a guiding star,
Illuminating the choices that will take me far.

With strength and courage, I'll challenge what's known,
Through vulnerability, I'll let my true self be shown.

Metamorphosis

No longer held back by fear's heavy chain,
I begin to break free from the mundane.

Pure intentions reveal my path and show me the way,
As I take steps with purpose and seize each new day.

When I'm stuck at a crossroads, choosing left or right,
I trust that my intuition will bring me to the light.

Feeling the love I hold deep inside, I no longer hide,
For I am ready to take on the world with pride.

A universe filled with treasures I have yet to dream of,
Awaits outside of this shell, calling for my love.

Breaking free from the egg that once held me tight,
I will find my truth and shine with all my might.

With each step forward, I'll create my own fate,
Guided by intention, I'll manifest a life that is great.

I will no longer live in a haze,
That blurs together all of my days.

In the pursuit of dreams, I'll find my bliss,
With my heart as my compass, I'll never miss.

I choose to believe that I am loved and protected,
Even though sometimes I feel lonely and rejected.

Those feelings arise from the darkness in me,
But that doesn't mean that I have to agree.

I choose love, and I choose light,
And I refuse to give up this fight.

I choose to not let others influence how I feel,
So that I can control my emotions and begin to heal.

The Egg

Majestic Consciousness

In the landscape of my mind, a transformation takes place,
As I reshape my thoughts and create a new space.

I have wandered too long through a barren terrain,
Where negative whispers fuel doubt and pain.

But now I stand tall, with resolve in my gaze,
Ready to reshape my mental maze.

I banish the doubts that once held me back,
And use declarations that keep me on track.

Gone is the hesitation, the "I can't" and "I won't,"
As I replace them with words that have a positive tone.

I release the grip of negative thinking's hold,
And stop listening to the stories my thoughts once told.

"I can" becomes the anthem that resonates within,
Empowering me to conquer, to rise, and to win.

No longer held back by self-imposed limitations,
I begin to believe in myself and taste true liberation.

"I get to" replaces "I have to" in my vocabulary,
A shift in perspective through newfound clarity.

With gratitude, I recognize life's abundant gifts,
And the opportunities that await as my spirit lifts.

Affirmations become my allies, supporting my light,
As I speak them with conviction, both day and night.

No longer will I be drained by negativity's toll,
For I choose thoughts that nourish my soul.

Metamorphosis

"I am worthy," I declare, with unwavering belief,
In my goals, my dreams, and the love I receive.

I am the architect of my mental landscape,
I get to mold it into a joyful escape.

Thought by thought, I reshape my inner terrain,
As I crack the shell and break free from the pain.

With every affirmation, I strengthen my core,
And get ready for the dreams that knock at my door.

The old thought patterns crumble away,
Creating space for me to grow each passing day.

Affirmations become steppingstones, leading the way,
As they help me escape from the egg that kept me at bay.

I choose thoughts that uplift, inspire, and motivate,
That transform my mindset and transmute my fate.

No longer bound by the chains of anxiety and despair,
I glimpse into the light and breathe in fresh air.

In developing conscious structures, I am free,
To become the best version of who I am meant to be.

I am more than capable, more than enough,
The light within me expands; it knows I am tough.

With each positive thought creating a crack in the shell,
I will unveil a world where endless possibilities dwell.

With each new day, a fresh canvas I see,
To paint with colors that set my spirit free.

No longer confined by doubts that drain,
I begin to change my story and release my pain.

The Egg

Embryonic Diapause

In suspended development, emotions reside,
A tempest within that seeks to divide.

I have given them power; they have been in control,
But now they prevent me from healing my soul.

No longer will I be helpless, adrift in the storm,
I'll step back and find the energy I need to transform.

No longer held captive by their fierce command,
I begin to rise above the chaos and take a stand.

I acknowledge and observe, with a curious eye,
The triggers that set my emotions awry.

I analyze the ideas and beliefs that fuel the fire,
And extinguish the anxiety as my brain rewires.

External circumstances cannot stress me,
For I know I'm exactly where I'm supposed to be.

I delve into the depths of my thoughts and fears,
And unravel the threads that have caused tears.

At the core lies a wounded part of my being,
That longs for healing and for a new way of seeing.

I acknowledge the feelings that arise each day,
And through understanding, I find a better way.

With gentle compassion, I hold them near,
Through them, my true self becomes clear.

I inhale the light and exhale the dark,
As I transform the turmoil and ignite a spark.

Metamorphosis

I reclaim my power, my sovereignty,
No longer swept away in the sentimental sea.

Feelings ebb and flow, like tides in the night,
But I remain steady, anchored in my light.

No longer enslaved by their fierce sway,
I let them pass through, for I know they won't stay.

I observe them with calmness as they drift by,
No longer controlled by the tears that I cry.

I am in control, and I can rebuild my soul,
By welcoming my emotions until I feel whole.

I am not defined by any emotional tide,
I stand as the observer, with calmness inside.

Understanding the waves, I chart a new course,
And sail my boat beyond the emotive force.

Emancipated from their gripping hold,
I continue my voyage, courageous and bold.

I am ready to step into the unknown,
As I begin the next phase that's yet to be shown.

I am the master, the captain of my ship,
Navigating emotions with love's tight grip.

I will steer my feelings toward a new shore,
Until I arrive at a land containing dreams to explore.

With every breath, I release what no longer serves,
I honor my emotions, their purpose observed.

My journey unfolds as I let go of the past,
And look forward to the future, ready to be free at last.

The Egg

Hatching

In the egg of my mind, I have been confined,
But I have found a way to freely unwind.

There is a power lying dormant, eager to be unfurled,
Capable of releasing my authentic self into the world.

I recognize the limitations that held me tight,
And with newfound awareness, they show me the light.

No longer confined by walls of my own making,
I continue my voyage of self-discovery through awakening.

I release the chains that held me in place,
And I allow self-love to keep me in its embrace.

Making peace with the darkness, I find strength within,
Enough to shatter the barriers and let a new phase begin.

No longer controlled by the tides of my emotions,
I rise above the current and overcome their motions.

The waves may come, but I stand strong and tall,
Conquering my thoughts, I learn to ride them all.

I reclaim the reins, steering my life's direction,
As I unleash my power with unwavering conviction.

Like a larva emerging, I shed my old skin,
And reveal the power that I hold deep within.

I will explore the world, wide-eyed and free,
A symbol of rebirth, of the person I am meant to be.

With legs that will carry me, I will reach new heights,
And leave behind the shadows as I witness new sights.

Metamorphosis

I will step into the unknown, into uncharted grounds,
And I will search until my inner light is permanently found.

For I am the architect designing my destiny,
Guided by the strength that now flows through me.

I will take responsibility for my own well-being,
By no longer caring about what others are seeing.

Stepping beyond the egg that kept me contained,
I venture forth into a land that is untamed.

No longer held within my mind and body's shell,
I emerge as a new being, ready to excel.

I was lost in the dark, but now I see,
The only person getting in my way was me.

I am ready to let go of who I used to be,
As I use the present moment to set myself free.

Continuing my voyage of self-realization,
I align with my higher self in cosmic perfection.

I'll let the world behold the beauty that lies within,
A radiant being that is ready to thrive and win.

My light is calling me, asking me to give it my all,
And to live life authentically as I learn to crawl.

As I break past the limits that I once knew,
I begin to live a life that is no longer blue.

I hatch from the egg, feeling reborn and brand new,
Ready to face the world with dreams to pursue.

With every breath, I acknowledge the divine,
And unleash the power that has always been mine.

PART II

The Larva

"You've gotta be a caterpillar before you are a butterfly. Problem is, most people aren't willing to be a caterpillar."

— Anonymous

"We are like larvae, awaiting the moment when we emerge as our true selves."

— Adam Weishaupt

The Larva

Learning to Crawl

In the next stage of metamorphosis, I find what I need,
As I nourish my soul with nurturing milkweed.

In this crucial phase, I must honestly believe,
That self-love is what I must achieve.

Like the larva cares for itself, preparing to transform,
I, too, must tend to my mind and body amidst life's storms.

I seek balance and rest that will help me replenish and mend,
So that I may create a space where my soul can transcend.

This crucial period of growth is a time to genuinely care,
For the foundation of a vibrant life, I must now lay bare.

No longer shall I neglect the temple that I live inside of,
No longer shall I make others responsible for giving me love.

I have relied on medications, seeking solace from without,
But true healing starts within; of that, there is no doubt.

The love I sought from others I will now give unto myself,
For only through self-love can I regain my inner wealth.

No longer dependent on external hands to make me whole,
I begin to take responsibility as the sole architect of my soul.

My mental landscape is a garden I get to sow,
I choose to water seeds of positivity so that they'll grow.

I will keep nourishing my mind with thoughts that inspire,
And feed my spirit so that my dreams can go higher.

Through meditation and mindfulness, I found a tranquil space,
To cultivate a healthy mindset and grow my inner grace.

Metamorphosis

In movement and in stillness, I'll tend to my physical frame,
With exercise and rest, I'll reclaim my vibrant flame.

A healthy mind and body, intertwined,
Lay the groundwork for a life that is aligned.

Together, they pave the way for a beautiful life to bloom,
As I honor my vessel, my transformation will surely have room.

I'll seek the sunlight's warmth and connect with nature's embrace,
Allowing its beauty to fill my heart until it starts to race.

For in the storms of life, I'll find solace and peace,
As I nurture my well-being and let my worries cease.

Just as the larva thrives when it is cared for and attended,
I, too, shall emphasize self-care, ensuring I am mended.

I will learn to prioritize rest, rejuvenation, and play,
So that I am ready for the challenges that come my way.

With determination in my heart and strength in my stride,
I will take care of this being in which I reside.

My body deserves to be loved, adored, and cared for,
And it starts with me making choices that are better than before.

I reclaim the power to shape my own fate,
I can always take responsibility, for it is never too late.

I will improve my well-being,
As I take over my own healing.

I embody the truth that love starts within,
A quiet sanctuary where self-compassion can begin.

No longer seeking outside for what is truly mine,
I will cultivate self-love, a treasure that is divine.

The Larva

Calm Amidst the Storm

In learning to crawl, I learn to roam,
And I get lost trying to find my home.

In this bleak labyrinth, I must find my way,
Through the storms of life that lead me astray.

Moments of doubt carry whispers in the breeze,
But I remain connected, one with all that breathes.

Breathing in, breathing out, I find solace within,
And use mindfulness to calm storms before they begin.

I learn to get comfortable with doing nothing,
So that my body knows I am here, listening.

Breathing mindfully, I reroute my attention,
I focus on my body and give it affection.

As I feel each heartbeat in my chest,
I let my body know that it is okay to rest.

Stress may surround me, but I just breathe,
I calm the storms and allow myself to be.

In the realm of less, I discover more,
Filling my cup right at my core.

I ride the waves of stress, letting them ebb and flow,
For I know that every storm must eventually go.

With patience and trust, I will weather it all,
And emerge victorious, standing proud and tall.

The ocean is vast, and challenges will arise,
But with calm observation, I will be more wise.

Metamorphosis

Within sacred pauses, I recharge my light,
So that I may navigate through the depths of the night.

The minutes need not be optimized in haste,
For time is a companion, not a race to be faced.

Through mindfulness and trust, my spirit will mend,
As I find the calm amidst the storm and my soul transcends.

When I get scared, I remember the truth that is profound,
Though the storm may rage, I will remain safe and sound.

I am not defined by labels, thoughts, or perceptions,
My being cannot be contained within an expression.

For I am not defined by my body,
I am the force within, pure energy.

In this web of life, we are intertwined,
A collection of energy, beautifully designed.

I need not fear; for I know I am never alone,
I am connected to all, a part of the unknown.

The universe's creation is in a cosmic trance,
As I try to find my role within this galactic dance.

Within this grand tapestry, woven with care,
Every thread finds a purpose; every strand is laid bare.

As a larva, I fear not the trials I may face,
Finding inner stillness, I will face them with grace.

I know that I am doing my best to handle life's tests,
And soon, I will pass, and my soul will be able to rest.

I will no longer keep fighting the tides,
Instead, I will learn to enjoy the ride.

The Larva

Caterpillar's Call

In the hustle and bustle of life's endless race,
I have come to learn the value of slowing my pace.

Storms pick up speed, craving productivity's bliss,
And they leave me feeling stuck in exhaustion's abyss.

I release the urge to fill each moment with haste,
The thoughts that say I must be productive are erased.

My body whispers, my mind gently speaks,
They call for self-love, for the healing they seek.

They ask that I listen to my own needs,
And that I care for my being by watering my seeds.

Self-care can be a relaxing walk outside,
Where nature's display becomes my guide.

The rustling leaves and the calming breeze,
Whisper secrets that put my mind at ease.

Under the warm sun, I bask in its gentle caress,
A moment of stillness, a chance to decompress.

When panic begins to spread across my chest,
My spirit shows my mind and body how to rest.

It is only thinking that makes life seem bad,
By shedding my thoughts, I no longer feel sad.

I stop engaging with what brings suffering,
And focus instead on the light that is growing.

Every closed door leads me to a window,
And it is up to me which path I choose to follow.

Metamorphosis

I choose to allow my being the freedom to flow,
As I release all tension and let my worries go.

Caring for myself makes my heart sing,
As I listen to the desires that echo and ring.

Through awareness, I find the balance to thrive,
And I connect with myself until I start to feel alive.

Just ten minutes a day is more than enough time,
To check how I am doing and help my thoughts align.

I turn to my journal and the world disappears,
As I capture my emotions, dreams, and fears.

No longer shall I hide behind the excuse,
That self-care is a luxury I must refuse.

My well-being is my treasure, my utmost priority,
For when I am not well, life loses its clarity.

In these moments of tranquility, I find my way,
As I replenish my energy and shine brighter each day.

I begin to flourish like a flower in bloom,
Radiating the best version of me as I cast out gloom.

No longer a slave to the rush and the grind,
I forge a new path with clarity of mind.

I now know how to be better than before,
By caring for myself like I am something I adore.

Through these acts of self-love, I replenish my soul,
And connect with the parts of my being that yearn to be whole.

With love and compassion, I nurture my inner flame,
As I recharge and get ready to play this game.

The Larva

Larval Harmony

Within self-care, there is a quest to align,
My mind, body, and spirit with the divine.

I know that the reason I haven't felt whole,
Is because I've been neglecting parts of my soul.

As a larva, I seek to live life wholeheartedly,
As I make inner peace, love, and wisdom a part of me.

But to find true fulfillment and a sense of serenity,
I must align with my values and find inner harmony.

By taking full responsibility for my well-being,
A sense of purpose emerges from within my being.

Inner peace, like a tranquil river, begins to flow,
Cleansing my thoughts as I let negativity go.

As I sit in the stillness, I find my way,
Feeling stronger and better with each passing day.

Within the tranquil silence, I find serenity,
A respite for my soul, a chance to just be.

I soak in the quietude and begin to feel calm,
Wounds start healing, for peace is a soothing balm.

Love, the eternal flame, ignites my very core,
Radiating kindness and compassion that I can't ignore.

I thirst for knowledge; there is a yearning to grow,
So, I expand my horizons and challenge what I know.

Learning becomes the compass that leads the way,
As I say yes to the side quests that arise each day.

Metamorphosis

In my feelings, actions, and thoughts, a symphony I find,
A harmonious existence in my heart, body, and mind.

The orchestra of life begins to play, oh so sweet,
Guiding me with ease through each of my heartbeats.

In this dance of existence, a melody comes to light,
As my soul begins to dance with pure delight.

The cosmic song brings me deeper within,
And my skin tingles with adrenaline.

There is peace and love unlike what I've known,
As my inner light allows itself to be shown.

Peace reverberates as I flow through life's stream,
In harmonic resonance as I fulfill my soul's dream.

No longer a struggle but a gentle, effortless sway,
I live in alignment and find peace every day.

With each breath, I surrender to life and go with its flow,
Knowing that living wholeheartedly, I will find my glow.

I never know what tomorrow might bring,
So, I will just focus on letting my heart sing.

In taking care of myself and slowing down,
I honor the stillness where peace is found.

The tides are high, and the waters are tough,
Helping me sparkle like a diamond in the rough.

Soon, it will be time for me to shine,
For no one can take this self-love of mine.

Until then, I will continue to crawl along,
Listening to the melody of this divine song.

The Larva

Gentle Warrior

As a larva, I must face the dangers outside,
As I learn to fight with love by my side.

In the realm of resilience, a warrior emerges,
Not wielding a sword, but a heart that surges.

My heartbeat is strong, but it is also tender,
I become vulnerable as I learn to surrender.

It takes immense strength to let walls crumble,
To expose my tender heart, knowing I may stumble.

With love as my armor and compassion by my side,
I tread upon the path where authenticity resides.

No longer encased in an egg's protective shell,
I dare venture forth with my story to tell.

For love and care, they hold immense might,
As they reveal my courage and banish fear from sight.

In this vast world, where battles may ensue,
I learn to be patient until my spirit breaks through.

In practicing empathy, I find a new way,
To be resilient and grow stronger each day.

As a gentle warrior with a heart open wide,
I create a space where no one needs to hide.

I become a luminary as I continue along and listen to the song,
And I extend grace to those that feel like they don't belong.

For they, too, seek solace, their own battles they fight,
Together we can rise and show one another the light.

Metamorphosis

We all feel suffering and pain during our lifespans,
As we continue to do the best that we can.

I give others the compassion I have cultivated,
And hope that their pain is alleviated.

Endurance stems from love's patient embrace,
With kindness as my fuel, I pick up the pace.

In moments of doubt, when strength seems thin,
I hold steadfast, for I know that love will win.

With my armor of love, I show my might,
As I navigate this world from morning to night.

I will keep doing what I believe is right,
So that I may continue to align with my inner light.

In loving others, and myself, as I do,
I emerge triumphant and live a life that is true.

The world reflects back at me what I hold within,
And it is up to me which emotions I allow in.

When I give out kindness, I receive kindness back,
As I give my love freely, for it is something I never lack.

I learn how to care for my tender, loving heart,
Knowing it is a source of strength, a precious work of art.

What I previously saw as average and unremarkable,
Has now become the source of my sparkle.

So, let me be a warrior, gentle and kind,
In a world that often forgets that love is what binds.

In love's eternal presence, I will find my way,
With patience and endurance, come what may.

The Larva

Molting

Through action and movement, I find a cause,
As I change and leave behind who I once was.

Making my way across a land that is unknown,
I find various tests where my strength is shown.

No longer a chore but a time of delight,
I engage in motion, and my spirit takes flight.

As I begin to move, I find a new love affair,
From running, to walking, to dancing through the air.

A chemical cocktail of endorphins floods my veins,
And unleashes the energy that my inner light contains.

As the sun rises, I stretch and greet the day,
Using yoga to find balance in each step of the way.

I long to someday reach the sky,
But first, I need the strength to fly.

I hear nature's call, and I go for a walk,
Listening to the birds as they each talk.

I know that one day, I will join them in the trees,
Until then, I'll settle for the peace carried in the breeze.

Hiking through mountains, I let down my hair,
As I venture away from trails without a care.

I begin to see the world from a new height,
Further encouraging me to take flight.

Through neighborhoods, I explore each street,
With every stride, I feel my heart's steady beat.

Metamorphosis

Through every beat of my heart, my spirit lifts,
Endorphins are unleashed, giving me a gift.

This secret, this energy, is a present I have found,
A natural high connecting me to all that is around.

My body now feels healthier than before,
And I feel like I can take on so much more.

My mind is calm as I continue to move,
Feeling joy as my mood starts to improve.

Exercise is the catalyst that allows me to endure,
As I build perseverance and make my spirit pure.

With every step, every breath, I grow,
And I show up as my best self, ready to glow.

Every bead of sweat cleanses my spirit,
As I take care of this body that I inhabit.

As I molt old habits and begin to feel alive,
My body feels light, and my passions thrive.

I celebrate my life and dance with glee,
As I feel the endorphins that help me succeed.

The chemicals ignite my soul's fire,
And help me pursue what I desire.

Through finding new movements, my gift unfolds,
As I unleash my power and break the molds.

I will keep dancing in this symphony divine,
Where exercise and endorphins intertwine.

For in its rhythm, I surrender to the flow,
And help my strength and spirit grow.

The Larva

Restoring Energy

Alongside movement, there is a path I must tread,
Seeking foods that nourish and help me get out of bed.

I must care for myself inside and out,
For health is a treasure, of that there is no doubt.

I pay attention to how I fuel my vessel,
And take loving care of it, for it is a miracle.

I feed my body whatever it needs,
As a growing larva, I search for milkweed.

Long gone are the days of seeking solace in sweets,
For true nourishment lies in nature's own treats.

Baking was my refuge; it helped me escape anxiety's embrace,
But pounds piled on as I became depressed in my tired haze.

Lethargy consumed me and drained my very core,
And I knew I had to become healthier than before.

Now, I've discovered how to make my body happy,
By consuming nourishment that agrees with me.

With creativity, I cook and savor each bite,
Taking pleasure in nutrition, a newfound delight.

Veggies burst with vitality, a powerhouse of life,
They nourish my body and banish fatigue's strife.

With newfound wisdom, I prepare my meals with care,
Enhancing their flavors, I make them a joy to share.

No longer do I seek comfort solely in taste,
But in the nourishment held in each bite that I take.

Metamorphosis

No longer a mere consumer, I become aware,
Of what I eat and if it is grown with care.

Food brings more than pleasure; it can make me strong,
It is a pathway to wellness where I can't go wrong.

In each bite, gratitude blooms and mindfulness shines,
As I am aware of the energy that grows on vines.

I honor my body, the vessel that I possess,
By fueling it with goodness and treating it no less.

I honor the environment in a sustainable way,
For mindless consumption has left it in disarray.

I commit my plate to hold foods that uplift,
That fill me with vitality and give my spirit a gift.

Nourishing joy resides in what I consume,
As I do my best to support my beautiful bloom.

With every bite, I encourage the best version of me,
As I create the energy I need for a life filled with glee.

I show myself and the planet love and care,
For we both desire growth and repair.

Through conscious nourishment, I've found my way,
As I choose foods that sustain me throughout the day.

Providing for my body, mind, and soul,
Is a mindful and loving act of self-control.

Each bite helps restore my energy,
As I continue to pursue my destiny.

I want to see just how great life can be,
And that will require delving further into me.

The Larva

Bonds of Belonging

With energy restored, I now yearn to find,
A place where my entire being can intertwine.

In this dance of existence, I search for a way,
To build a home within, where my spirit can play.

A sanctuary where I can reveal my true face,
Where my spirit can soar, and my soul finds its grace.

In moments of uncertainty, I am overwhelmed and lost,
Leaving me to search for refuge at any given cost.

When anxiety clouds the path ahead,
I yearn for a place where my soul can be fed.

I seek a place to rest my weary bones and find reprieve,
A place where solace resides so that my heart may receive.

With patience and bravery, I navigate the unknown,
I trust in the universe and follow a path unshown.

Amidst the chaos that creates strife,
I find a place of stillness to recalibrate life.

Within the stillness, I discover a haven so sweet,
A sanctuary of belonging where my soul finds retreat.

For in the depths of my being, a home awaits,
Where my spirit can soar, and my heart celebrates.

By surrendering to the universe, I find my home,
A treasured space within where I am never alone.

Amidst life's ebb and flow, I forge a sacred bond,
A communion with myself that allows me to go beyond.

Metamorphosis

I listen to the call of my spirit, to the whispers of my soul,
And find solace and peace as I learn to play my role.

I surrender to life's rhythm, its mystical embrace,
And I accept the present moment as I find comfort and grace.

For true belonging lies not in the external world,
But in the depths of my being, where my true self unfurls.

I sing my song freely as I let down all of my walls,
There is only my beating heart here, where love gently calls.

I anchor my roots in accepting myself all around,
And I create a home where true peace is found.

Within these bonds, there is a profound connection,
That helps me find liberation in a haven for reflection.

In this safe dwelling, I lay down my strife,
As I witness the beauty that comes with life.

I relax and surrender to life's current sway,
Knowing that within me, I will always find my way.

I trust that my intuition will tell me what is right,
It knows what my mind, body, and spirit need to be all right.

No longer a wanderer lost in the fray,
I find my way within, where peace is destined to stay.

The voyage of self-discovery is profound,
As I unravel the beliefs that once kept me bound.

Let me continue my trip with the love I hold inside,
Nurturing the bonds of belonging where peace resides.

For in the depths of self-discovery's delight,
I find the power to unveil my inner light.

The Larva

Pre-Pupation

As I continue to reveal my true face,
I transition into my own sacred space.

I separate myself from the world and delve within,
And I uncover the power that will help me win.

I will create a cocoon that is just for me,
A place where my authentic self can be.

For deep within the chambers of my soul,
I will find what I need to become whole.

With courage and compassion, I embark on this quest,
Seeking an inner landscape where my soul can rest.

Authenticity beckons, its voice a gentle plea,
It invites me to explore, to truly be free.

In the quietude of self-reflection's grace,
I shed the masks and the illusions I face.

For too long, I have played roles, wearing a disguise,
But now it is time for my true self to rise.

No longer bound by fear's crippling hold,
I will emerge with colors that are strong and bold.

By following my higher self's bliss,
I find the strength to accept my uniqueness.

Each step is a revelation, a potent seed,
That nurtures the strength I need to proceed.

By seeking, I will unearth the real me,
A soul that is untamed, vibrant, and free.

Metamorphosis

As I commune with my higher self, a discovery unfolds,
Destroying the illusions of the stories I have been told.

No longer confined to society's mold,
I stand tall, authentic, and uncontrolled.

The worry of judgment begins to fade,
As I honor my truth, completely unafraid.

I continue to satisfy seeking's sacred art,
And find the strength to mend my fragmented heart.

As I find a place to hang, life becomes clear,
And I shed the shackles of doubt and fear.

No longer chained by the need to fit in,
I can finally be myself and stop playing pretend.

I have the wisdom to navigate this course,
And to forge my own path back to source.

The world may question, doubt, and misunderstand,
But my inner truth prevails, like a lighthouse in the sand.

Nurturing my essence, I will rise anew,
And my inner light will shine brilliantly true.

The strength I hold within is not in force or might,
But in the courage needed to surrender to the light.

I will be brave as I continue the expedition within,
Discovering the power that resides beneath my skin.

So, let me enter the cocoon where I am in control,
As I embody the strength that lies in my soul.

I will seek with passion, with purpose, and with grace,
As I unveil my light and enter my authentic space.

PART III

The Pupa

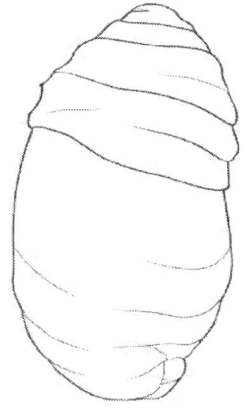

"Adding wings to caterpillars does not create butterflies.... Butterflies are created through transformation."

— Stephanie Marshall

"When you find yourself cocooned in isolation and you cannot find your way out of darkness... Remember, this is similar to the place where caterpillars go to grow their wings."

— Necole Stephens

The Pupa

Awakening Chrysalis

Enveloped within the pupa's gentle embrace,
I seek further transformation of my inner space.

Through authentic passion and purpose, I aim to find,
What makes my heart sing and brings peace to my mind.

I delve into the memories of my childhood days,
When joy was abundant in the simplest of ways.

For the light that stirred within my youth,
Brings me dreams and glimpses of truth.

The games that I played, the tales that I spun,
All of the things that I loved, where have they gone?

Those childhood pleasures were pure and free,
And they will lead me to who I am meant to be.

Through painting, writing, exploring, and more,
I partake in the activities that my spirit adores.

Singing, dancing, and the art of creation,
Each bring me closer to my soul's destination.

I learn to decode the whispers of my spirit,
As I realize my purpose upon this planet.

I listen closely to the songs of my heart,
And let them guide me, for they will never depart.

In these moments of pure delight,
I align with my higher self and shine bright.

Every endeavor has a purpose to be found,
Each is a vessel to spread my light around.

Metamorphosis

I delve deeper into the depths of my soul,
Where the flames of my true passions take control.

In the space between no longer and not yet,
I honor myself, and all my needs are met.

Awakening in this chrysalis, I am closer to my core,
Where my purpose and light will help me soar.

The knowledge I unearth through endless quests,
Will help me show up as my absolute best.

The things I enjoy more than others might,
Will help me unlock my inner light.

I reflect on how these activities make me feel,
How they mend my spirit and help my wounds heal.

I dance to the rhythm of my own heartbeat,
And sing the melodies that make my soul complete.

With every step, I feel the light drawing near,
And my authentic self becomes more clear.

In the presence of what supports my soul's love,
I find the strength that will help me rise above.

From inside the pupa's gentle cocoon,
I'll nurture the passions that make me swoon.

One day I'll emerge, transformed and free,
And I'll unleash my light for the world to see.

But first, I must proceed with my sacred quest,
To discover the joys that bring my soul rest.

In the search for what makes my heart sing,
I will find the peace that will turn into wings.

The Pupa

Whispers of Transformation

Searching for authenticity, I arrive at a new shore,
Where I connect with myself and open inner doors.

I step beyond the boundaries of what I already know,
And venture into uncharted realms where possibilities grow.

With an open mind and heart, I chart the unexplored,
For it is in untraveled territories that wisdom is restored.

Behind the closed doors, I leave behind my conditioning,
As I question who is in my head, always listening.

I wonder who I am when it is just me,
When I let my guard down enough to just be.

Who am I when there aren't others to please,
When all of my false selves are released?

Only with no one and nothing around,
Am I able to go where my inner light is found.

With each step that I take, I find treasures to behold,
Experiences that shape me as new stories are told.

The places I will go to are for me to decide,
As my strengths and creativity collide.

With each new endeavor, my horizons expand,
As I discover new passions, guided by curiosity's hand.

I find joy in exploration, in viewing new perspectives,
In unlocking hidden talents to meet my new objectives.

Curiosity becomes my lifelong companion and guide,
A beacon of light that fuels my eternal stride.

Metamorphosis

As long as I remain curious, I will continue to learn,
Constantly evolving as I seek knowledge at every turn.

I draw inspiration from the work of those that are wise,
Their creations and contributions help me open my eyes.

Observing their brilliance, I pause and reflect,
As I accept the truths that others may reject.

I absorb their wisdom, their artistry, and skill,
Discerning what resonates and what aligns with my will.

In this realm of endless possibilities, I find fulfillment,
As I create a life that leaves me in amazement.

I attract the pursuits that align with my soul,
And I support them wholeheartedly, making them my goal.

I reroute the endeavors that no longer serve,
For self-care is vital, and my being I must preserve.

Transformation burns within; it is a constant flame,
An alchemical fire that fuels my unique aim.

With each new interest, I uncover a new part of me,
For I am constantly evolving and removing old debris.

On this quest of curiosity, I find my true name,
As I accept myself fully and let go of any shame.

In caring for my being, I let go of what does not ignite,
And I nurture the flames that illuminate my inner light.

In the endless pursuit of knowledge and innovation,
I continue this adventure of discovery and transformation.

Within these walls, I clearly hear my heart's song,
And it has been patiently waiting for me to sing along.

The Pupa

Ethereal Beginnings

In the vast expanse of life's grand scheme,
I am on a quest to find my own gleam.

As I witness every breath-taking scene,
I begin to wonder what my life may mean.

I search for a path to follow, for a purpose to unfold,
As I continue a voyage where my inner light shines bold.

But life's meaning is not predetermined nor set,
I can always change my mind and decide to reset.

No single truth, but a myriad of paths to explore,
I pursue tales of purpose that resonate at my core.

I yearn to let my light effortlessly shine,
To banish the darkness that I once called mine.

Removing the prism that skewed my light,
I see through the colors that clouded my sight.

Gone are the filters and the masks that I wear,
For I know now what it is like to be truly aware.

Seeing myself as an observer of the universe,
Any remaining fear is removed, then put in reverse.

The feelings of panic that fed my anxiety,
Are now turned into love of every variety.

I fall in love with all aspects of life,
Even the ones that once brought me strife.

For darkness was needed in order to see,
The light that has always been inside of me.

Metamorphosis

With universal love, I set my light free,
And become one with all that can ever be.

I let the universe carry me away,
And I rest in peace, knowing all will be okay.

With ease, I allow my soul to freely flow,
And its love helps me share my vibrant glow.

No longer burdened by the weight of existence,
I embody abundance through love's sweet assistance.

Soon, I will overflow with self-love's gentle grace,
As I fulfill a purpose which transcends time and space.

I seek the activities that let my love freely express,
For they help my burdened heart decompress.

The moments that put me in a state of flow,
Strengthen my inner light and help it grow.

As I am flowing, I am one with the cosmic sea,
Here, time dissipates, and I am boundlessly free.

In these moments, I glimpse the universe's song,
And feel interconnected, knowing I am where I belong.

Listening to its melody, I shed my falsehoods,
As I realize I am a leaf on a tree in the middle of the woods.

Thoughts cease and I am one with all that is,
Connected to the galaxy where boundless beauty lives.

In my search for meaning, I find my own truth,
Unveiling the purpose that originated in my youth.

In the cocoon, I shine effortlessly, bright, and clear,
And I dismiss the darkness that I once held near.

The Pupa

Gratitude's Radiance

As I allow myself to be enveloped in the cocoon's embrace,
I find gratitude that leads to a transformational space.

For in its warm hold, I am led to see,
The abundance that surrounds you and me.

In this trip of existence, I pause to reflect,
On all my blessings, both subtle and direct.

I am grateful for the opportunities that come my way,
For the lessons I've learned shaping who I am today.

Gratitude allows me to see life's treasures,
It is a catalyst that brings boundless pleasure.

It illuminates my path by igniting my inner fire,
And it allows me to find peace as my heart feels lighter.

In this pupa stage, where change takes its hold,
I cherish the moments that are new and old.

With each breath, I am filled with amazement,
As I witness the wonders that are never absent.

When I focus on appreciation, I find,
A collection of miracles, both loving and kind.

Not everyone reaches this stage, this sacred phase,
Where they can prioritize their growth in a safe space.

When it feels like I am at the end of my rope,
I cling on to gratitude, for it brings me hope.

I am grateful for the abundance I have witnessed,
For the life I've been given and the things I hold dearest.

Metamorphosis

With its ups and downs, its twists and turns,
I find beauty in this game where my soul learns.

I am grateful for the challenges that strengthen my resolve,
And for the hard situations that help my spirit evolve.

Overcoming the threshold guardians of my soul,
I find my inner light and become whole.

Through journaling, mindfulness, and heartfelt praise,
I begin to open my heart wider in loving displays.

With each passing moment, my gratitude expands,
As I witness the miracles held within my hands.

I am grateful for this gift, the tapestry of life,
For it contains wisdom in its joys and strife.

I now see that all the suffering I have felt,
Was just a way to make my heart melt.

My walls needed to be broken down to the ground,
So that the light within me could be found.

The pain that I felt was a matter of perspective,
There was never anything truly defective.

Problems and drama created out of fear,
Are met with awareness, and they disappear.

I will continue my voyage with a heart full of grace,
In gratitude's radiance, I will find my rightful place.

Within the cocoon's compassion, I have found the key,
To unlock the abundance that I am meant to see.

For abundance abounds when I open my eyes,
And bask in the blessings that life provides.

The Pupa

Pupal Love

Gratitude opens the door and sets my heart free,
Allowing me to learn how to love unconditionally.

I love without judgment, without holding back,
For accepting others as they are is an affectionate act.

Through acceptance, connections are made,
Barriers begin to dissolve, and souls find their aid.

Holding compassion and forgiveness near,
I let my guard down and reject all fear.

In every situation, I allow love to be my guide,
As I shine the light that I have found inside.

I must not forget to show myself love as well,
Self-love is the cornerstone that allows me to excel.

In the sanctuary of universal love, I find my release,
As the voice within, my friend, whispers in peace.

No longer an enemy, but a companion that is dear,
My thoughts are now free, and I no longer live in fear.

Unconditional love is the essence of the divine,
It is interwoven into the grand design.

It makes life worth living; I listen to its call,
As I promote peace and unity for one and all.

By loving all unconditionally, I find,
A state of peace within my mind.

I surrender to life's flow with arms open wide,
And accept all that comes as I ride love's tide.

Metamorphosis

Burdens are lifted, and my spirit soars,
For love's radiant light opens all doors.

Within my cocoon, I take a sacred vow,
To care for myself and others, here and now.

I love without conditions or a sense of possession,
As I recognize the light in others without question.

Loving all that I meet is life's greatest gift,
It brings peace that allows my spirit to shift.

It unites hearts in harmony, dissolving all divides,
And creates a safe space where world peace can reside.

In each interaction, each breath that I take,
I use unconditional love to keep me awake.

Within the depths of its indiscriminating care,
I discover the beauty of life that is always there.

I can give myself the love I have been dreaming of,
By treating myself like a gift sent from above.

I remind myself that I am special and worthy,
And I appreciate every part of my journey.

Through love, I will find my righteous place,
As I unravel the layers and reveal my true face.

Loving unconditionally brings me to a higher state,
It is a gift I can share with the world as part of my fate.

I am ready to break free from my comfort zone,
For I realize there is more to life than what I've known.

The fragments of my heart are welded with gold,
As I find my purpose and become a sight to behold.

The Pupa

Transcending Perspective

Through love, my thoughts become a work of art,
As I shift my gaze, ready for a brand-new start.

In the alchemy of perspective, a new tale unfolds,
As I control my narrative and change the stories told.

Challenges emerge as gems in disguise,
For they allow me to see where wisdom lies.

With a positive mindset, I forge a new way,
Refusing the thoughts that bring shadows into play.

By changing my thoughts, I shape my inner view,
And release the notions that once made me blue.

I choose uplifting frequencies, thoughts that inspire,
And in their radiant glow, I become what I admire.

A transmutation occurs, allowing me to mend,
As I harness the power to ascend and transcend.

Recognizing the beliefs that anchored me down,
I release their grip through the wisdom I've found.

In the absence of darkness, anxiety fades,
As I walk a path where love and light pervade.

No longer bound by the weight of despair,
I rise above and breathe in the celestial air.

Gravity no longer pulls me to the ground,
As I get ready to fly with the love I've found.

Soon, I will leave my ego and go beyond form,
As I use this cocoon to fully transform.

Metamorphosis

I refuse to believe in the tales of gloom,
As I water the seeds that help hope bloom.

The greatest relationship I will have is with myself,
By loving who I am, I fall in love with life itself.

I am the alchemist of my own reality,
I can craft a world infused with vitality.

No longer a slave to darkness, I break free,
As I use love and wisdom to fulfill my destiny.

With every shift in perspective, a new dawn unfurls,
Revealing the beauty that lies all over the world.

Even in the bleakest moments that come my way,
I remind myself that there will always be a better day.

Through positive thinking, I will get a positive outcome,
For that is all part of the universe's algorithm.

The seeds that I water with my attention,
Will eventually blossom and come to fruition.

So, let me always see the silver lining's gleam,
The beauty that resides within life's intricate scheme.

Through the alchemy of the self, I find the key,
To unlock my higher self and set her free.

By doing what I feel is absolutely right,
I become one with my inner light.

In every situation, there is a lesson to uncover,
As I choose to perceive life as full of wonder.

By transcending my perspective, I forge ahead,
And transform the darkness into light I can spread.

The Pupa

Wing Development

In the face of life's tempest, fierce and wild,
I find solace in a mindset that is gentle and mild.

It is within this power that I am made strong,
As I learn to nurture optimism when things go wrong.

In a world that tests resolve through unstable grounds,
I possess the power of positivity that freely abounds.

Life's trials may come, relentless and tough,
They test my determination and call my bluff.

But with a positive mindset, I stand tall,
Unyielding to the storms as I pursue my call.

In a world consumed by negativity's reign,
I choose to rise above and break the chain.

Using positivity to guide my inner light,
I begin to grow wings and get ready for flight.

While others succumb to the depths below,
I will do my best to let my heart glow.

I choose to stay afloat, buoyed by my own thinking,
As I ride the waves skillfully instead of sinking.

I rise with grace, soaring on love's wings,
As I overcome the challenges that adversity brings.

I see all hardships as an opportunity to grow,
To make the most of life's ebb and flow.

Every storm that comes will be a chance anew,
To learn, to grow, and to discover what is true.

Metamorphosis

In the midst of chaos, I will find my stride,
And use positivity to navigate the tides.

I seize each moment as a canvas to create,
A masterpiece that spreads love instead of hate.

I want to help others inspire and uplift,
As we share with one another our gifts.

With kindness and compassion, I navigate life's terrain,
And nurture a positive mindset, a shield against pain.

I no longer know what is up or down,
I just feel the light that is all around.

The doors of my soul have been opened wide,
And I welcome all who wish to come inside.

Let the storms rage on, with fury untold,
I shall navigate them with a spirit that is bold.

The power of positivity resides in me,
And it guides me through life's tumultuous sea.

With the power I hold, I can conquer all,
Overcoming each stumble as I stand proud and tall.

In the face of adversity, I am unwavering,
For the power of positivity is truly liberating.

And so, I trek on, with a heart so bright,
Nurturing optimism as I share my light.

With every step, I choose to be free,
As I welcome life's challenges with positivity.

In the face of darkness, I will rise above,
And cultivate light through life's endless love.

The Pupa

Authentic Coloring

In a world of conformity, where masks are often worn,
I choose to accept my true self the way I was born.

I will let my essence shine, radiant and bright,
Embodying my authentic self with all my soul's might.

Though others are weary of those that are different,
I choose to be my authentic self, for I am magnificent.

The things that set me apart and make me unique,
Are not meant to be hidden but encouraged to speak.

In my thoughts and emotions, I hold my own view,
As I revel in the beauty of being authentically true.

Every aspect of my being is embraced anew,
A reconciliation with myself that was overdue.

From the way I look to the loves that I hold dear,
The things others see are not always as they appear.

I see the world as colorful, whereas others see it as gray,
I discover hidden wonders where others find disarray.

Through my own lens, I perceive the world's grand design,
And find beauty in the mundane, treasures that are divine.

In the depths of my soul, a wellspring resides,
It unveils the realm where magic abides.

I tailor and mold my life to fit my own design,
By being who I am meant to be, no longer confined.

In the tapestry of life, I bring forth a vibrant thread,
Weaving through the mysteries where others may tread.

Metamorphosis

I discover hidden wonders in the overlooked and small,
As I become my authentic self and answer destiny's call.

Through authenticity, I deepen my connection,
And align my mind, heart, and spirit with pure intention.

In this pupa stage, I choose to be me,
As I prioritize myself so that I may be free.

I dance to the rhythm of my own beating heart,
As I express my truth and create my unique art.

No longer hiding in the shadows, I come out,
I leave the depths of my being as my heart shouts.

As I accept my true self, I find my way,
And I live in harmony, shining brighter each day.

In the depths of vulnerability, I uncover my might,
As I let all the walls come down and radiate my light.

I celebrate my quirks, the strengths I possess,
And love my authentic self, no longer suppressed.

For in my uniqueness, I find my soul's calling,
A hologram of light, beautifully enthralling.

As I connect my mind, heart, and spirit as one,
I become my true self, and the metamorphosis is done.

When I am true to myself, my soul's purpose is revealed,
A path is illuminated, where my spirit's longing is fulfilled.

With authenticity embodied, I will soar and excel,
As I become who I am meant to be, with a story to tell.

To break free, I act upon my highest interest and try my best,
And I listen to my heart while the universe handles the rest.

The Pupa

Eclosion

As I listen to my higher self's gentle call,
I begin to break down the cocoon's walls.

No longer shall I wait for external love to arrive,
Instead, I will use self-love to help me thrive.

With tender patience and love, I nurture my own soul,
No longer waiting for someone else to make me whole.

The world's clock may tick, uncertain and finite,
But I will not cling to regrets in the fading twilight.

The Earth may cease its turning at any given moment,
Therefore, I will listen to my heart and make my atonement.

I shed the layers, the masks I wore,
No longer defined by what came before.

I forgive the moments of hiding, the years of disguise,
I now understand it was fear that clouded my skies.

I am the light I have been searching for,
And in this life, I need nothing more.

No longer shall I withhold compassion from my own heart,
Through unconditional love, I have discovered a sacred art.

I now realize the importance of self-care,
As I love myself fully and tend to the wounds I bear.

I release the fear of judgment that once held me back,
As I push against the cocoon and hear it crack.

I forgive myself for neglecting my own needs,
For putting others first while my own soul bleeds.

Metamorphosis

Contemplating my existence, I grant myself grace,
And I let go of past sorrows as I create a loving space.

For how could I have shared my love if I knew not its touch,
If my own heart was void and I asked of others too much?

I now see the truth in loving myself completely,
I comprehend that I'm the only one who can complete me.

With empathy and understanding, I find liberation,
As I follow the radiant path that leads to self-realization.

By tending to my wounds and nurturing my flame,
I awaken the compassion that bears no shame.

With an open heart, I offer kindness to myself and those around,
For I know that through compassion, unity is found.

With every act of kindness, forgiveness, and care,
I cultivate a love that is boundless and rare.

So, I listen to my heart as I continue on my way,
Knowing that the love within me will always stay.

With self-compassion as my steady companion,
I am ready for self-discovery and union.

In being who I am, both gentle and strong,
I nurture a love that will carry me along.

As I love myself deeply, unconditionally, and fully,
I share my boundless love generously with those that I see.

By cultivating compassion, I learn what love truly means,
And from that sacred wellspring, I share its vibrant streams.

I will walk this path, creating a life that is new,
As I honor the beauty of love that is true.

PART IV

The Adult

"Nature's message was always there and for us to see. It was written on the wings of butterflies."

— Kjell B. Sandved

"Just when the caterpillar thought the world was over, it became a butterfly."

— Chuang Tzu

The Adult

Through the Cocoon's Veil

Within the safety of my cocoon, I found solace,
As I transformed and unveiled my true face.

Now, I can emerge as a butterfly and reach for the sky,
With wings spread wide, I am ready to fly.

No longer confined, I break free,
And shed the fears that once bound me.

I once blamed others for my stagnant state,
Not realizing that I control my own fate.

Deep within, the power has always been mine,
I can uncover the truth and let my light shine.

I was weighed down by expectations for too long,
And the weight that I carried made me strong.

I will navigate this world as I shine my inner light,
With every step, I will show my authentic might.

The excuses I made, the limits I believed,
They were but illusions, a web of lies that I weaved.

Now I see the truth clear as day,
I hold the power to pave my own way.

On this new Earth, there is nothing to fear,
For I now see there is only love here.

With love in my heart, unconditional and pure,
In my own skin, I start to feel secure.

Mind, body, and spirit, in harmony and aligned,
Reveal a life that is beautifully designed.

Metamorphosis

No longer lost in the shadows of the past,
I step into the light, boldly, at last.

Unveiling my true self, I finally see,
That I always had the power to set myself free.

I release the doubts, the fears that bind,
Finally seeing the beauty within my mind.

The energy of my true self begins to flow,
As I take flight and let my inner light glow.

I listen closely to my heart's sweet song,
It is the spirit that has been there all along.

In tune with the whispers of my soul,
I fulfill my needs and make myself whole.

I will let the world witness my magic flight,
As I dance in the wind with colors that are bright.

Finally feeling like my true self, I no longer roam,
Now that I am a butterfly, I have found my true home.

As I unveil my essence, I am set free,
Knowing I am the person I was meant to be.

I have unmasked the layers and revealed my core,
And now the world is mine to explore.

I fly with purpose, freedom, and grace,
Embodying my true self as I find my place.

My first flight could end in a fall,
But I will keep trying to answer my call.

For life is great and beautifully abundant,
When I allow myself to be carried in its current.

The Adult

Celestial Wings

In this newfound freedom, I find my way,
As I live wholeheartedly in a world of disarray.

The world keeps burning as it is turning,
But I won't let the smoke keep me from flying.

I pause and reflect on what truly matters,
Listening to the whispers of my wing's soft flutters.

In living with purpose, intention, and care,
I find a path that leads to joy beyond compare.

I align my thoughts, actions, and desires,
With the values that fuel my inner fire.

Unconditional love, originating from within,
Helps extend my compassion so that we all may win.

Others reflect back at me the energy I provide,
As we begin to realize we are on the same side.

By assisting others and helping them shine,
We all get one step closer to the divine.

I have discovered the secret to a life well-lived,
By creating a life where my heart can give.

Through giving, I open myself up to receiving,
As I mend the wounds that needed healing.

I let my heart lead in all that I do,
And I trust the path that feels true.

I honor my values; they illuminate my way,
As I create a life of purpose where I can play.

Metamorphosis

Authenticity shines as I stay true,
And live in alignment with what I pursue.

I release the need to fit in and conform,
And embrace my uniqueness in its full form.

I no longer feel the need to impress,
For in my essence, I find my happiness.

Loving what was once an insecurity,
I have reached the final stage of maturity.

I now see that to be high, I first needed to be low,
Now, I can let go and be carried in life's flow.

I dance with the shadows that I still see,
And I accept them all as a part of me.

With kindness and empathy, I reach out my hand,
Creating connections through a web that expands.

In the heart of humanity, we are all one,
A collection of souls, right where we belong.

In valuing kindness, I nurture more than my soul,
I create ripples of love that make the world whole.

I choose peace over chaos, serenity over strife,
So that I can begin to create a balanced life.

I walk with integrity, my goals in sight,
As I live my truth and become the light.

With a heart open wide, I let my values shine,
And I create a world where genuine connections thrive.

With gratitude, I welcome each day's embrace,
And trust that life will unfold with perfect grace.

The Adult

Colors in Flight

As I have discovered myself, I've begun to see,
How to honor the boundaries that define you and me.

A sacred dance between myself and others,
As we each become our own authors.

Listening to my inner voice, I learn to say no,
Releasing the fear of disappointing those I know.

For in setting clear boundaries, I grant myself peace,
And I respect the needs that help me find my release.

Old habits now fade as I bid them farewell,
And I live a life filled with new stories to tell.

People-pleasing tendencies are blown by the breeze,
And I pursue a new beginning with courage and ease.

Making room for the things that are meant for me,
I love myself fully and set my true self free.

I make my boundaries firm and clear,
And I do not waver on what I hold dear.

Through my choices and actions, I create my existence,
As I use each moment to decrease my resistance.

How I care for myself will set the stage,
As my story continues to unfold upon each page.

If I want a world of kindness, I must lead the way,
By treating myself adequately each passing day.

With every boundary I set, I strengthen my being,
And I empower my body and soul, a feeling so freeing.

Metamorphosis

By honoring my limits, my truth takes flight,
And authenticity shines its radiant light.

I hold myself dear, with love and with care,
As I value the unique essence that I bear.

Upholding the boundaries that others may set,
I can make choices that I will not regret.

In showing others the respect they are worthy of,
They show me the same and share their love.

Everyone deserves to have their own space,
A place that allows them to show their true face.

Within my own boundaries, I unfold and grow,
And I remain true, no matter where I go.

My mind, body, and spirit work together,
Allowing me to fly in the breeze, light as a feather.

My thoughts and emotions are no longer heavy like lead,
There is finally peace in my mind when I lay in bed.

I admire self-respect like stars in the night,
A constellation of self-love that shines pure and bright.

I feel myself beginning to fly higher,
As I use my boundaries to fuel my inner fire.

In honoring myself, I discover my light's true gleam,
A beautiful display that makes life feel like a dream.

My goals are waiting to come to life,
They offer me a way to deal with strife.

I start creating a new way of living for my being,
As I use my light to make something worth seeing.

The Adult

Rise of the Monarch

As I fly through the air without a care,
My soul feels light, unburdened, and aware.

No longer hiding behind a veil of false displays,
I am ready to start anew without any delays.

I let myself shine beautifully and true,
As I attract kindred spirits that align with my hue.

When my guard is down, I focus on what is around,
And my mind begins to turn into a playground.

In this world, I can be anything and everything,
And the reality I live in is of my own making.

Life is about creation through exploration,
As I unleash the power of my imagination.

I dream of a place where all find their light,
For that is when Earth will finally feel all right.

Mindfully, I care for this light that I hold,
And I invite others to join as their own stories unfold.

Authenticity becomes the bridge that we cross,
As we create bonds that can weather any loss.

Through vulnerability, our souls intertwine,
As we share our dreams and shape the grand design.

By showing up as my authentic self, I ignite,
A spark that inspires others to shine their own light.

My vulnerability creates a space where all may glow,
A place of belonging where genuine connections grow.

Metamorphosis

In this dance of vulnerability, we unveil,
A realm where deep connections may prevail.

True relationships emerge from the core,
Fostering love and support that will help us soar.

With open hearts, we can lend a helping hand,
To those that feel stranded in this land.

I support others as their journeys take flight,
And I find inner peace as darkness turns to light.

For authenticity begets authenticity, you see,
Creating a ripple effect in which we are all set free.

Residing in a safe haven where masks dissolve,
We can reveal the beauty within as we all evolve.

In this sacred space, our true selves unfold,
As we change the stories that we once told.

Hand in hand, we bridge the gaps we find,
And build relationships that help our hearts align.

We share, we listen, and we empathize,
As we foster a community where everyone thrives.

Let us all celebrate the power of being real,
As we break down our walls and share how we feel.

In the safety of acceptance, our true strength is revealed,
No longer bound by judgment, we are free to be healed.

We can create a sanctuary where masks need not reside,
A space where all are welcomed, where no one needs to hide.

I will be a pioneer, with authenticity as my song,
As I manifest a world where everyone can belong.

The Adult

Unveiling Splendor

Where connections thrive, there is a symphony of souls,
As we celebrate our differences, knowing we each play a role.

Basking in the beauty of diversity, I find my inspiration,
A kaleidoscope of colors that paints the entire nation.

We each have coloring that is uniquely profound,
By accepting our differences, true beauty can be found.

There is no need to conform or hide my glorious hue,
For in accepting myself, my spirit shines through.

And as I honor my being, I honor others too,
For their quirks and perspectives add to life's view.

There is no shame in being who I am; I have my own voice,
In a world that tells me to play along, I have a choice.

While some may seek to fit in, blend, and conform,
I choose to stand proud amidst a crowd that is uniform.

I am done trying to fight the person I want to be,
My light has been unveiled for the world to see.

By not conforming to societal norms, I shine my light,
And I celebrate who I am as I illuminate the night.

Diversity is the spice of life, the essence of our way,
It fuels innovation and designs the paths that we lay.

In the symphony of souls, I find universal grace,
As each unique voice leaves a lasting trace.

We are each a part of the grand design,
Weaving tales of wonder as our stories intertwine.

Metamorphosis

In this world of contrast, we can all merge and interlace,
As we use diverse minds to shape the human race.

So, celebrate the weirdness, the things that set you apart,
For in embracing your truth, you ignite a fiery spark.

And as we cherish diversity, let us build a world that is fair,
Where all perspectives matter, and we show that we care.

By celebrating diversity, we foster love's expanse,
And together, hand in hand, we can all dance.

Instead of focusing on what sets us apart,
We can each focus on the beating of our hearts.

We are all human; that is easy to see,
So, let's create a world where we can all agree.

A world where differences are set aside,
Because we respect the light we each hold inside.

We can mend the world and forge new alliances,
By focusing on what unites us and loving our differences.

By changing the ideas that we choose to believe,
We can change the reality that we all perceive.

We are all trying to survive, to shine our own light,
So, let's make sure that we are treating each other right.

Sharing our compassion will help others fill their cup,
As we create a world where no one wants to give up.

Many are lost at sea, drowning as they try to find their way,
And they need someone to tell them that it will be okay.

We can all fight for the world we wish to see,
And it all starts with you and me.

The Adult

Eternal Beauty

As a butterfly, I take flight and find my new stride,
And I soar through the sky with a thirst I cannot hide.

The world is my classroom, an endless sea of wonder,
A treasure trove of knowledge, calling me to discover.

I become one with the breeze, seeing no end in sight,
I surrender and let the wind carry me like I am a kite.

I no longer feel the urge to resist what is,
When I accept life's flow, I find inner bliss.

Knowing there are no labels to define me,
I no longer care about what others may see.

Anxiety is a feeling that no longer resonates,
For I have merged with the light that illuminates.

My thoughts are now guided by awareness,
And they seek the truths that lead to fairness.

I have made peace with my own history,
Now it is time to take on life's mysteries.

Through this world, I now begin to travel,
Going beyond paths paved by gravel.

I choose to make the most out of the hand I've been dealt,
Regardless of how I may have previously felt.

No limits can contain me as I flutter through the air,
Seeking new perspectives with an insatiable flair.

My mind is open like the sky, with no clouds in sight,
For I know that everything will be all right.

Metamorphosis

I turn to the ancient writings where wisdom resides,
Words penned by sages and scholars, timeless guides.

Their ink-stained pages whisper secrets of the past,
They share lessons learned about how nothing ever lasts.

Yet, it is not just the echoes of history that I seek,
But the stories of those around me, for every voice is unique.

Within their shared experiences lies a wealth untold,
A storybook of narratives waiting to be told.

And in this digital age, where knowledge knows no bounds,
I delve into the virtual realm, where infinite wisdom can be found.

With a click and a keystroke, the world is at my command,
I search for new frontiers and ideas as I navigate this land.

Though I have taken flight, I know my trip's not complete,
For growth knows no conclusion, it is an eternal feat.

With every passing moment, a chapter is unfurled,
I am always changing as I explore this wondrous world.

As I navigate through life's space, I seek growth and learning,
For knowledge and truth can satisfy my heart's yearning.

Each beat guides me as I continue my journey,
Flowing through this world abundantly.

I do my best to praise myself and support my endeavors,
Because my light shines brighter when I love myself better.

I am proud of the person I have become,
Even though my transformation has barely begun.

I know that investing in myself will pay off,
Because I now know what I am made of.

The Adult

Flying Toward Destiny

As I soar through the sky, I am whom I am meant to be,
Letting go of the past, I fly toward my destiny.

In the depths of my being, there are seeds that I sow,
Of love, compassion, and empathy, and I watch them grow.

I tend to my inner garden with attentive care,
Nourishing the blossoms that are delicate and rare.

For they are not treasures to seek afar,
But creations of my heart, shining like a star.

Each points me on my way through this land,
As I feel the light inside of me expand.

I turn inward to the wellspring within,
Where love's gentle current effortlessly begins.

With love, I water the seeds and quench their thirst,
Adding compassion to the soil where empathy is immersed.

I nurture self-love in my tender embrace,
And I accept my flaws with kindness and grace.

I have made peace with the skeletons in my closet,
For I know I am not meant to be perfect.

As love fills my cup, it begins to overflow,
And my spirit awakens with a warm, gentle glow.

I see the world through empathetic eyes,
And understand others beneath their disguise.

I listen with care to the stories they hold,
As I create a space where hearts can unfold.

Metamorphosis

Through gentle acts and words, I share my light,
Becoming a beacon in the darkest of nights.

For love, compassion, and empathy will help me,
As I continue to heal throughout my journey.

With open hearts, we can bridge the divide,
And build a kinder world, side by side.

In every room, my presence will shine,
A light of understanding, divine and benign.

As I pour love upon my soul's terrain,
It seeps into the cracks and soothes my pain.

In this caring act, we all can partake,
As we mend our societies, for all of our sakes.

Let us all nurture love, compassion, and empathy,
Not as distant dreams, but as part of our legacy.

When we approach others with open hearts,
We heal and unite, and a new Earth starts.

When we radiate these gifts from within,
We create a world where love can win.

Even though I am just one butterfly,
I can still create storms across the sky.

One flap of my wings can change the planet,
As my light begins to cover it like a blanket.

It all starts with the love I show when I'm alone,
For all delightful things are homegrown.

I will keep filling my cup throughout the day,
So that I am ready to pave a new way.

The Adult

Graceful Evolution

Originating within my vibrant soul,
Love allows my creativity to be in control.

After being lost in the dark, I find a light,
That yearns for ways to share its might.

There are projects that beckon, calling my name,
They invite me to fuel the imaginative flame.

With gifts and passions, I am blessed,
They stoke the fire that burns within my chest.

In the dance of creation, I find my flow,
A timeless rhythm where inhibitions go.

I find my source of inspiration, an artist's dream,
As I express the light that makes my heart gleam.

From the depths of my mind, they arise,
Ideas that ask me to break free from disguise.

In this vast world, where wonders reside,
I answer their call with my heart open wide.

A rhyme that dances upon my tongue,
A tune that allows my song to be sung.

Experiments address the curiosity that is burning,
Eagerly, I research the questions that life brings.

The world is a canvas of endless allure,
That beckons me to explore and to endure.

In each brushstroke, I reveal my truth,
Colors swirl and remind me of my youth.

Metamorphosis

My heartbeat no longer whispers; it has grown strong,
It now invites me to leap, to go where I belong.

In moments of flow, time drifts away,
As I surrender to my muse's gentle sway.

The truest version of me finally unfurls her wings,
Coming out to play after years of hiding.

With each stroke, each note, each rhyme,
My inner light shines, going beyond space and time.

Through creativity, I can truly express,
The depths of my being, the secrets I possess.

I let go of resistance, of holding back,
And I find peace knowing I am on the right track.

My body is at ease and my thoughts are set free,
As I create a channel for my inner light to be.

Creativity is a river that is pure and clean,
And it flows with the magical beauty I've seen.

In its current, I am led to explore,
As I connect with the world that I adore.

By nurturing my gifts, my divine spark,
I can brighten the world with a luminous arc.

Creativity is the key to expressing my soul,
As I share the truths that make me whole.

For as I express, and let my essence unfurl,
I find my solace in exploring this world.

Through creativity's abundant flow,
I share my light and help others find their glow.

The Adult

Unfolding the Mystery

In the depths of despair, I've known the weight,
Of a soul that feels alone, left to fate.

But I fought the waves and found solace on the shore,
As I transformed the darkness into something more.

I let the universe take my worries and fears,
For I have shed more than enough tears.

When I find myself getting upset or stressed,
I focus on all of the ways that I am blessed.

Listening to the birds singing outside,
I begin to set my thoughts aside.

I trust that things will unfold as they are meant to,
So, I let go of my thoughts and enjoy the view.

Though there may be things out of my control,
I get to choose how I respond and how I play my role.

From egg to larva, from pupa to butterfly,
I've tasted transformation, and I've learned how to fly.

I created a cocoon, a sacred space to bloom,
Which helped me emerge as an adult without gloom.

With wings unfurled, I seek to spread my light,
To guide those lost as they yearn for insight.

I strive to make a difference, wherever I may be,
By touching aching hearts and setting weary spirits free.

I have known the darkness, the shadows' hold,
And now that I am free, I want to help others unfold.

Metamorphosis

No boundaries restrict my compassionate quest,
To ease burdened hearts and offer them rest.

In this world, where pain and sorrows dwell,
I can help others escape their self-made cells.

My heart is yearning for unity and peace,
For a home where all souls find solace and release.

I long for Earth to be a place where all can belong,
For it to be a sanctuary where souls can grow strong.

I will not falter or yield in this meaningful fight,
To create a better world where darkness turns into light.

Together, as beautiful butterflies, we will soar high,
And let our unique colors paint the sky.

We can all keep going, never losing sight,
Of the things that make us feel all right.

For we hold the power to heal and ignite,
As we craft a world where souls shine bright.

Let us make a difference, one act at a time,
Embracing compassion as we let our hearts chime.

In this quest for a better world, I will share my light,
Until we all can soar like butterflies in flight.

Through compassion and creation,
We can each find our inspiration.

There is more to living than just being alive,
As we find our inner lights, we can all thrive.

Like a phoenix, from the ashes we will rise,
As we use our wings to become more wise.

Epilogue

As I reach the end of this metamorphic quest,
I look back upon all the ways I have been blessed.

From the humble egg to the butterfly's flight,
Metamorphosis has shown me its wondrous might.

But growth and self-realization never truly cease,
For it is a lifelong endeavor to maintain inner peace.

The path I follow is not linear; challenges may arise,
Yet with courage and resilience, I've become more wise.

Breaking free from limitations that once held me back,
I nurture my well-being and get on the right track.

Finding my inner light, I shine it with grace,
And I invite others into the divine's embrace.

The world eagerly awaits your gifts and light,
As you spread your wings and take flight.

Trust in your potential and let your brilliance unfurl,
As you unveil your inner light and release it into the world.

This is not the end, dear reader, but a fresh start,
For now, I must go on to play a new part.

With an open heart, I will navigate life's terrain,
Experiencing growth as I learn from joy and pain.

In moments of uncertainty, I will be gentle and kind,
Grateful for all of the opportunities that I find.

I now know I possess the power to create,
A life filled with purpose that is genuinely great.

Metamorphosis

I ask that you love every ounce of your being,
For every inch of you is worth seeing.

Make a best friend out of the voice in your head,
Having it on your side will help you get ahead.

Listen to your body and all of its needs,
As you do your best to water positive seeds.

Allow the beating of your heart to guide you,
As it leads you toward a life that is true.

Never forget the spark that you hold,
A piece of the divine worth more than gold.

Shine your light in a world that is dark,
And never let anyone dim your spark.

Open your heart as you receive inner peace,
And surrender to the universe so that life is a breeze.

Be mindful of the beliefs that you allow in,
The boundary between light and dark is paper thin.

Believe that all is all right, and all is okay,
And do not let anyone or anything ruin your day.

What you choose to do is all up to you,
I hope you succeed in what you wish to pursue.

Let your metamorphosis begin as you unveil the light within,
For life is a game, one that we can help each other win.

Play it with love, compassion, and determination,
And use your wings to change the nation.

With heartfelt gratitude, I bid you adieu,
Good luck creating a life that is unique to you.

Acknowledgments

Thank you to those who helped me become who I am today,
For guiding me through the dark and helping me find my way.

Thank you for assisting with my metamorphosis and learning,
It is because of you that I now have wings to go flying.

Gracias por todo.

Made in the USA
Monee, IL
26 September 2024

825c2835-fb92-4e38-b64b-cff90472072bR01